The Prayer Rule of the Theotokos

of

Saint Seraphim of Sarov

Chi Rho Publishing

Table of Contents

History of The Prayer Rule of the Theotokos

Very little is, indeed, known about the history of the Prayer Rule of the Theotokos. There is a tradition that the Egyptian monks of the Thebaid prayed 150 Angelic Salutations grouped into 15 groups of ten, after the pattern of the Psalms. Beyond this, what we do know has come down to us from a certain Father Zosima. He was a spiritual son of the great 19th Century Russian Orthodox saint, Seraphim of Sarov (1759-1833). Here is the message left to us from the holy priest, Father Zosima:

> I forgot to give you a piece of advice vital for salvation. Say the Rejoice, O Virgin Theotokos one hundred and fifty times, and this prayer will lead you on the way to salvation. This rule was given by the Mother of God herself in about the eighth century, and at one time all Christians fulfilled it. We Orthodox have forgotten about it, and Saint Seraphim has reminded me of this Rule. In my hands I have a hand-written book from the cell of Saint Seraphim, containing a description of the many miracles

which took place through praying to the Mother of God and especially through saying one hundred and fifty times the Rejoice, O Virgin Theotokos. If, being unaccustomed to it, it is difficult to master one hundred and fifty repetitions daily, say it fifty times at first. After every ten repetitions say the "Our Father" once and "Open unto us the door of your loving kindness." Whomever he spoke to about this miracle-working Rule remained grateful to him.

The Prayer Rule as prayed by Saint Seraphim has come down to us by means of his notebook. A set of 15 meditations which embrace the whole life of the Theotokos was devised by Bishop Seraphim Zvezdinsky of Dmitrov. He prayed the complete fifteen-decade Rule daily and encouraged all Christians to do likewise. Murdered by the Communists in 1937, he is a Holy New Hieromartyr of the Russian Church. The decade meditations given here are those offered by Saint Seraphim Zvezdinsky. The prayers which follow each decade were composed by a nun who was a disciple of St. Seraphim Zvezdinsky.

The Prayers

Rejoice, O Virgin Theotokos Mary, full of grace, the Lord is with You. Blessed are you among women, and blessed is the fruit of Your womb, for you have born Christ, the Savior of our souls.

Our Father, Who art in heaven, hallowed be Thy Name.

Thy kingdom come, Thy will be done on earth as it is in heaven. Give us this day our daily bread, and forgive us our trespasses as we forgive those who trespass against us. And lead us not into temptation, but deliver us from the evil one.

For Thine is the kingdom and the power and the glory, Father, Son, and Holy Spirit, now and ever and forever. Amen.

Open unto us the door of your loving-kindness, O most blessed Theotokos. As we set our hope in you, let us not be confounded, but through you may we be delivered from all adversities. For you are the salvation of all Christians.

The Prayer Rule
Of the Theotokos

As Prayed by the great

19th Century Russian Orthodox Mystic,

Saint Seraphim

Of Sarov

In the Name of the Father, and of the Son, and of the Holy Spirit.

Amen.

O God, be merciful to me a sinner.

Glory to You, Our God, Glory to You!

O Heavenly King, Comforter, Spirit of Truth, everywhere present and filling all things, Treasury of blessings and Giver of Life: come and dwell within us, cleanse us of all stain, and save our souls, O gracious One.

Holy God, Holy Mighty, Holy Immortal, have mercy on us!
Holy God, Holy Mighty, Holy Immortal, have mercy on us!
Holy God, Holy Mighty, Holy Immortal, have mercy on us!

Glory to the Father, and to the Son, and to the Holy Spirit,
now and ever and forever. Amen.

O Most Holy Trinity, have mercy on us. O Lord, cleanse
us of our sins. O Master forgive us our transgressions.
O Holy One, come to us and heal our infirmities,
for Your Name's sake.

Lord, have mercy. Lord, have mercy. Lord, have mercy.

Glory to the Father, and to the Son, and to the Holy Spirit, now and ever and forever. Amen.

Our Father, Who art in heaven, hallowed be Thy Name. Thy Kingdom come, Thy will be done on earth as it is in heaven. Give us this day our daily bread, and forgive us our trespasses as we forgive those who trespass against us. And lead us not into temptation, but deliver us from the evil one.

For Thine is the kingdom and the power and the glory,
Father, Son, and Holy Spirit, now and ever and forever.
Amen.

Lord, have mercy. Lord, have mercy. Lord, have mercy.

Glory to the Father, and to the Son, and to the Holy Spirit,
now and ever and forever. Amen.

Come, let us adore the King our God!
Come, let us adore Christ, the King and our God!
Come, let us adore and bow down to the only
Lord Jesus Christ, the King and our God!

I believe in one God, the Father Almighty, Creator of heaven and earth, of all things visible and invisible. And in one Lord Jesus Christ, Son of God, the only-begotten, born of the Father before all ages; Light from Light, true God from true God, begotten, not made, one in essence with the Father, through Whom all things were made. For us and for our salvation He Came down from heaven and was incarnate of the Holy Spirit and the Virgin Mary and became man. He was crucified for us under Pontius Pilate, and suffered and was buried. He rose on the third day, according to the Scriptures.

He ascended into heaven and is seated at the right hand of the Father. And He is coming again in glory to judge the living and the dead and His kingdom will have no end. And in the Holy Spirit, the Lord, the Creator of life, Who proceeds from the Father, Who together with the Father and the Son is worshipped and glorified, Who spoke through the prophets. In one, holy, catholic, and apostolic Church. I profess one baptism for the remission of sins. I expect the resurrection of the dead, and the life of the world to come.

Amen.

O Lord, open my lips, and my mouth shall proclaim Your praise.

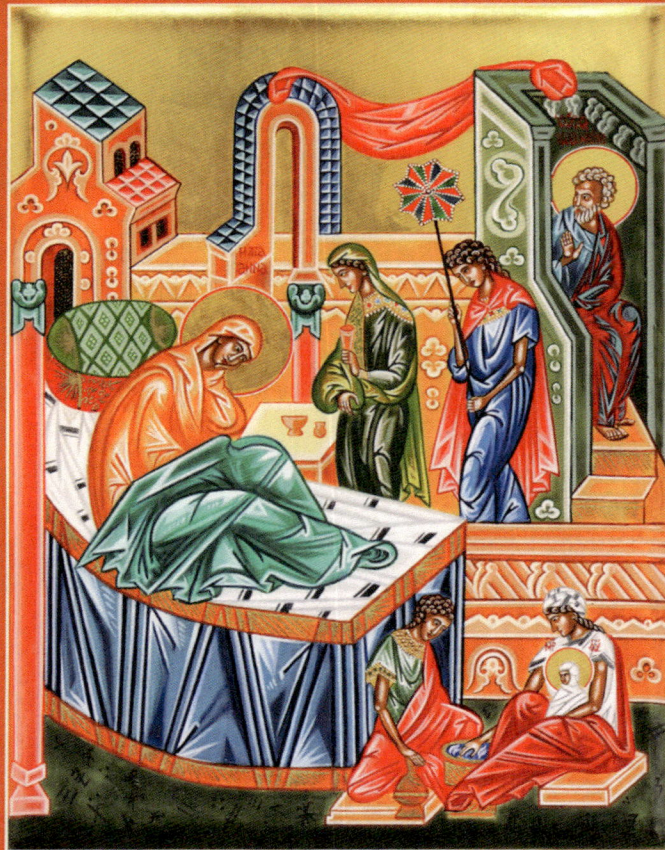

Let us remember the

Nativity of the Theotokos.
Let us pray for mothers, fathers and children.

Rejoice, O Virgin Theotokos... *(Ten times)*

Our Lady, Blessed Theotokos, save and preserve your servants (names of parents, relatives, friends), increase their faith and repentance, and when they die give them rest with the saints in your eternal glory.

Our Father, Who art in heaven...

Open unto us the door of your loving-kindness...

Let us remember the feast of the

Presentation of the Blessed Virgin and Theotokos.

Let us pray for those who have lost their way and have fallen away from the Church.

Rejoice, O Virgin Theotokos... *(Ten times)*

Our Lady, Blessed Theotokos, save and preserve and unite or re-unite to the Orthodox Catholic Church your servants who have fallen from the path and lost their way.

Our Father, Who art in heaven...

Open unto us the door of your loving-kindness...

Let us remember the

Annunciation of the Blessed Theotokos.
Let us pray for the soothing of sorrows and the
consolation of the those who grieve.

Rejoice, O Virgin Theotokos... *(Ten times)*

Our Lady, Blessed Theotokos, soothe our sorrows
and send consolation to your servants who are
grieving and ill (names).

Our Father, Who art in heaven...

Open unto us the door of your loving-kindness...

Let us remember the

Meeting of the Blessed Virgin with the Righteous Elizabeth.
Let us pray for the reunion of the separated, for those whose
dear ones or children are living away from them or missing.

Rejoice, O Virgin Theotokos... *(Ten times)*

Our Lady, Blessed Theotokos,
unite your servants who are separated.

Our Father, Who art in heaven...

Open unto us the door of your loving-kindness...

Let us remember the

Nativity of Christ.

Let us pray for the rebirth of souls, for new life in Christ.

Rejoice, O Virgin Theotokos... *(Ten times)*

Our Lady, Blessed Theotokos, grant unto me,
who has been baptized in Christ, to be clothed in Christ.

Our Father, Who art in heaven...

Open unto us the door of your loving-kindness...

ΜΡ ΘV

ΤΟΥΤ ΤΟ
ΒΡΕΦΟС
ΟΥΡΑΝΟΝ
ΚΑΙ ΓΗΝ Ε
ΤΕΡΕΟС

Let us remember the feast of the

Encounter of Our Lord with Simeon

and the words he uttered to the Theotokos: "Yea, a sword shall pierce through thine own soul also, that the thoughts of many hearts may be revealed." Let us pray that the Theotokos will meet our souls at the hour of death and will see to it that we receive the Holy Mysteries with our last breath, and will lead our souls safely through the toll houses.

Rejoice, O Virgin Theotokos... *(Ten times)*

Our Lady, Blessed Theotokos, let me receive the Holy Mysteries with my last breath, and lead my soul yourself through the trials of the toll houses.

Our Father, Who art in heaven...

Let us remember

The Flight of the Theotokos with the God~Child into Egypt.
Let us pray that the Mother of God will help us avoid temptations
in this life and deliver us from misfortunes.

Rejoice, O Virgin Theotokos... *(Ten times)*

Our Lady, Blessed Theotokos, help me avoid temptations in
this life and deliver me from misfortunes.

Our Father, Who art in heaven...

Open unto us the door of your loving-kindness...

Let us remember
The Disappearance of the Twelve Year-Old Boy Jesus in Jerusalem
and the sorrow of the Theotokos on His account.
Let us pray, begging the Mother of God for
the constant repetition of the Jesus Prayer.

Rejoice, O Virgin Theotokos... *(Ten times)*

Our Lady, Blessed Theotokos, grant to me the unceasing Jesus Prayer.

Our Father, Who art in heaven...

Open unto us the door of your loving-kindness...

Let us remember

The Miracle Performed at the Wedding in Cana of Galilee,
when the Lord turned water into wine at the words of the Theotokos:
"They have no wine." Let us ask the Mother of God for help in all
that we do and deliverance from all need.

Rejoice, O Virgin Theotokos... *(Ten times)*

Our Lady, Blessed Theotokos, help me in all my needs,
and deliver me from every need and sorrow.

Our Father, Who art in heaven...

Open unto us the door of your loving-kindness...

Let us remember

The Theotokos Standing at the Cross of the Lord,
when grief pierced through her heart like a sword. Let us pray to
the Mother of God for the strengthening of our souls
and the banishment of despondency.

Rejoice, O Virgin Theotokos... *(Ten times)*

Our Lady, Blessed Theotokos, strengthen my soul and banish my despair.

Our Father, Who art in heaven...

Open unto us the door of your loving-kindness...

Ἡ ἈΝΑΣΤΑΣΙΣ

Let us remember

The Resurrection of Christ

and ask the Theotokos in prayer to resurrect our souls and give us new courage for spiritual feats.

Rejoice, O Virgin Theotokos... *(Ten times)*

Our Lady, Blessed Theotokos, resurrect my soul and give us new courage for spiritual feats.

Our Father, Who art in heaven...

Open unto us the door of your loving-kindness...

Let us remember

The Ascension of Christ,

at which the Theotokos was present. Let us pray and ask the
Queen of Heaven to raise up our souls from earthly and
worldly amusements and direct them to striving for higher things.

Rejoice, O Virgin Theotokos...

Our Lady, Blessed Theotokos, deliver me from worldly thoughts
and give to me a mind and heart striving towards the
salvation of my soul.

Our Father, Who art in heaven...

Open unto us the door of your loving-kindness...

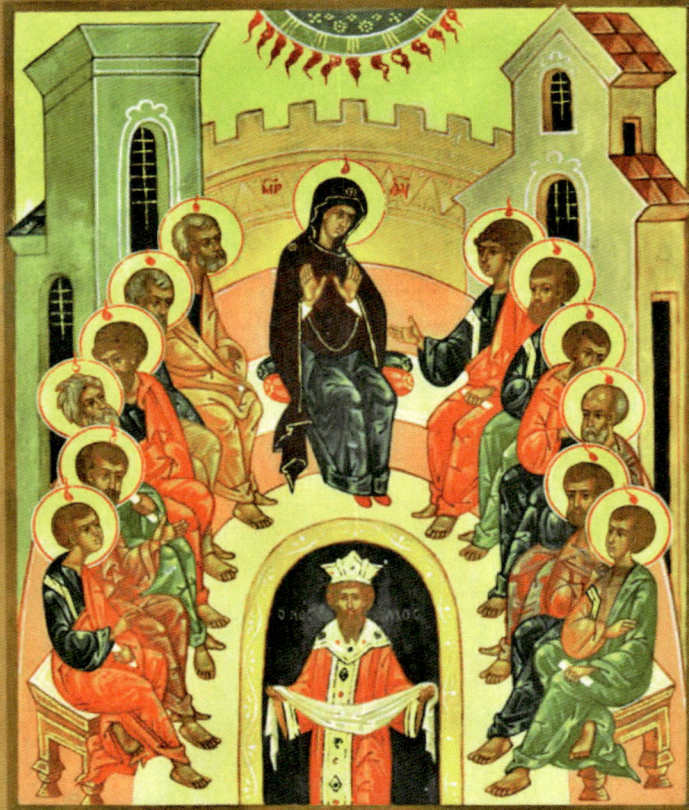
СОШЕСТВIЕ СТАГW ДХА

Let us remember the Upper Room and
The Descent of the Holy Spirit on the Apostles and the Theotokos.
Let us pray: Create in me a clean heart, O God; and renew a
right spirit within me. Cast me not away from your presence;
and take not your Holy Spirit from me.

Rejoice, O Virgin Theotokos... *(Ten times)*

Our Lady, Blessed Theotokos, make me a clean temple in which
God's Holy Spirit will ever dwell.

Our Father, Who art in heaven...

Open unto us the door of your loving-kindness...

Let us remember
The Dormition of the Blessed Theotokos,
and ask for a peaceful and serene end.

Rejoice, O Virgin Theotokos... *(Ten times)*

Our Lady, Blessed Theotokos, grant me a peaceful and serene end.

Our Father, Who art in heaven...

Open unto us the door of your loving-kindness...

Let us remember

The Glory of the Theotokos,

with which the Lord crowned her after her removal from earth to heaven. Let us pray to the Queen of Heaven not to abandon the faithful who are here on earth but to defend them from every evil, covering them with her honorable and protecting veil.

Rejoice, O Virgin Theotokos... *(Ten times)*

Our Lady, Blessed Theotokos, preserve me from every evil and cover me with your honorable and protecting veil.

Our Father, Who art in heaven...

Open unto us the door of your loving-kindness...

It is truly proper to glorify you, O Theotokos, the
ever blessed, immaculate and the Mother of God.
more honorable than the Cherubim and beyond compare
more glorious than the Seraphim, who a Virgin gave
birth to God the Word, you, truly the Theotokos,
we magnify.

Glory to the Father, and to the Son, and to the Holy Spirit,
now and ever and forever. Amen.

Lord, have mercy. Lord, have mercy. Lord, have mercy.

Through the prayers of thy Most Holy Mother, the Theotokos
and Ever-Virgin Mary, and through the prayers of our holy fathers,
and of all the saints, O Lord Jesus Christ our God,
have mercy on us.
Amen.